T0063520

SILENT THOUGHTS

CLASSICAL CHRISTIAN POEMS, RHYMES & QUOTES

"Thinking Is Life In Silent Motion"

Angus Dike

Order this book online at www.trafford.com
or email orders@trafford.com

Most Trafford titles are also available at major online book retailers.

© Copyright 2013 Angus Dike.
All rights reserved. No part of this publication may be reproduced, stored in a retrieval
system, or transmitted, in any form or by any means, electronic, mechanical, photocopying,
recording, or otherwise, without the written prior permission of the author.

Printed in the United States of America.

ISBN: 978-1-4907-1028-0 (sc)
ISBN: 978-1-4907-1027-3 (e)

Trafford rev. 09/20/2013

North America & international
toll-free: 1 888 232 4444 (USA & Canada)
fax: 812 355 4082

Silent Thoughts

Thoughts precede words
And thoughts precede deeds
To speak right, we think right
To do ill, we think ill
The thoughts of men I cannot read
But this much I know
Man's heart is deceitful
What do you think about?
In thoughts we spell our lives
And frame our destinies
In holy thoughts we write our names in gold
Higher than gold I prize my thoughts
For thinking is life in silent motion!

Dedication

This book is lovingly dedicated to my wonderful family of:
My beautiful wife: Akudo Uloma Peace Dike.,
My three wonderful kids—the 3Js: Jessica Chiemela, Jesse Tobenna and Joel Chinemerem.

Acknowledgement

My profound gratitude goes first to God for giving me the skill required for this work.

My lovely wife, Akudo Peace Dike and wonderful kids are warmly appreciated for their supports, prayers and encouragement.

My brother, Engineer John Dike and his dear wife are hereby acknowledged and appreciated for their supports.

My special thanks go to all members of Trafford team involved in this project, starting from May Brown, Jane Roberts, Mae Anderson, Jill Serinas and others.

Contents

Silent Thoughts v

Dedication vii

Acknowledgement ix

Contents xi

CHAPTER ONE

Sunset At Dawn —The Fall Of Man— 1

Before The Fall 2

The Deception 5

The Wilderness 7

Redemption 10

Last Note 11

CHAPTER TWO

—Love— 13

The Seed Of Love 14

True Love Never Dies! 14

Love Dynamics 15

Love is 15

God's Love Is 16

A New Heart 16

A New Song 17

Let Our Love Grow As The Years Go By 17

Vain Love 18

Love Melody 18

Walk in Love 19

The Angel Of Love 19

Love In Little Ways 20

All That Matters Is Love 20

Life Is Dynamic 21

Love Is A Weapon 21

Chapter Three

—The Word— 23

Chapter Four

Demons On Rampage 27

A: Demons Everywhere! 28

B: Fake Pastors, False Prophets And Phony Saints: 30

C: The Wise In Sin;—Godless Intellectuals; 32

D: Prostitutes, Sex Perverts And Nudists 34

E: Robbers And Killers, Kidnappers And Murderers 36

F: Idol worshippers, Cultists and Ritualists, Witches and Wizards, Voodoo Priests,
   Kings And Queens 39

G: Wicked Rulers, Corrupt Politicians, Officers And Officials 42

Last Note: 45

Chapter Five

Wisdom For The Wise 47

Teach Me To Be Wise 50

Chapter Six

Nuggets Of Truth 53

Chapter Seven

Warning Notes 63

. . . . Beware 63

The Running Tide 67

Chapter Eight

Life Is Like A Journey 69

Chapter Nine

Poems And Rhymes 73

Telling My Bride I'm Coming soon! 74

My Pledge 75

His Grace Is Amazing 76

Heaven Is My Home 76

A Heart Cry 77

The Hungry Soul 77

Sin 78

Beyond The Grave 78

Shadows Of The Real 79

Echoes From Above 79

The Brighter Side Of Life 80

He Set Me Free 80

Your Life As A Seed 81

I Need Time 82

The Voice Within 83

There Is A Mission To Your Life 83

Golden Thoughts 84

The Heart Diary 84

Who Can Save The Dead 85

The Face Behind The Wall 85

Life Is Not By Chance 86

Christ Makes the Difference 86

Watch And Pray 87

The Unwilling Captive 88

The Devil Can Not Stop Me 88

All That Is Mine For All That Could Be Mine 89

Life As A Mirage 90

Destiny As A Choice! 90

A Song From Above 91

He's Made All Things New 91

Live In little Ways 92

Resist The Stranger's Goods 93

We are Because He Is 94

The Bridge Of Life 94

This Day Is Not Mine.. 95

The Gift Of A New Day 96

To The Angel Of Love 98

Be My Bride... 98

Why Mind The Thorns When You Can Pick The Roses?..................... 100

Time Is Running Out... 102

Christ Is Coming Soon 102

The End Is Near 103

The Racing Tide 103

Night Time Calls 104

Chapter Ten

The Voice From Above—What Would Be Your Story?........................... 105

A 106

B: This Shall Be My story.. 110

C: 112

Chapter One

Sunset At Dawn
—The Fall Of Man—

Before The Fall

Moulded in divine artistry
Made in the image and likeness of God
Birthed in His eternal breath
Living in the garden of the Lord
I basked beside the crystal spring.

Clothed in celestial glory
Decked with gold, precious stones and pearls
A perfection of beauty, of wisdom and knowledge
An embodiment of all that is good, true and pure
I knew no sin.

Free and whole was my worship for Him
His word was mine to speak
His will mine to do
His life to live
As long as I was His.

With the garden as a home
Sorrows were far from me
Life was a sweet melody
A victory song—of joy, of peace and bliss
And sealed from want, I lived above the stars

With zests and fluency
Faith was my language
Love my first nature
In love all things were made for me
I for His glory.

My thoughts were sweet and pure
My ways good, just and true
Death was a strange word
Fear knew me not
As I saw His face all around and heard His voice above noisy waves.

My heart was in rapture
My soul was at peace
My body lacked no strength
My spirit ascended at will
And I knew no bounds.

I could not hate, hurt nor kill
I could not lie, cheat nor steal
Yes, I could not sin
Because I knew not how
His word was the food that made me grew.

His law was life
That life was a rich mine
Of knowledge, of wisdom and wealth
And the mine was mine
To mine at will.

I was the king of the earth
Subject to the King of kings
The lord of all
Subject to the Lord of lords
The monarch of all
Subject to the Maker of all.

At my rebuke the thunder calmed
At my voice the birds sang
The beasts heeded my call for silence
All was peace and bliss
The garden was a paradise
A semblance of heaven on earth.

The Deception

Then, one morning, so glorious, so dreadful
Came 'he' calling, with bags of tricks to trick
The fallen hero who sought to bring me down
The dissident who schemed to enlist my soul
The wicked one, he envied the life I had.

Lonely and sad he asked for a companion in hell
Cursed and damned, banned from the gates of life
Poor, wretched and sick, bruised and dead from defeat
His aim? To kill, to steal and destroy, all I was and had
And derail God's eternal plans.

He cowed and cajoled, he bewitched and beguiled
And I ate the fruit that poisoned my soul
The sin that ravaged my being
The deed was done and could not undo
Death was instant and would not reverse.

Suddenly all was void, black and blank
All night without a hope of day
It was a gamble, he won and I lost
God suffered no loss
His will was sure, His plans could not derail.

Like a candle in the wind, life was blown out
I was banished from my joyous home
The dwelling place of peace and plenty
Eclipsed from the sun of righteousness
For sin has entered the soul and damaged the heart.

Like a dream in the morning wake
As sunset at dawn
Life was all gone, vanished beyond the height of the soul
Swifter than the wind, faster than I could tell
Death set in as I exchanged God's immortal glory for a piece of berry.

The Wilderness

Then began I the descent into the abyss
An excursion into the wild world of sin
Strange spirits colonized my soul
Holding hostage the man within
Demanding a ransom I could not pay.

Swept ashore off the ocean of life
Driven from the garden of the Lord
Snowballed into the pit
Darkness engulfed my soul
For evil has found a home in me.

The stars receded
The moon recoiled
The sun seared
The earth quaked
The oceans surged, as the waters overflowed their banks.

The plants withered and the flowers faded
A whirlwind came, a tempest arose
The lions roared as the dogs barked
All creation rebelled against my soul
I had lost the mantle and great was the fall.

The floods came
As hails of tests around me rolled
Progress was in recess
Success in limbo and life in reverse
Friends swam away others grew wings and flew.

God's presence was all gone
His glory departed without a parting kiss
Leaving bare the soul
Exposing the man within
Down and beaten, weak and vulnerable to the wiles of hell.

All zest was gone
Trust turned to betrayal
Faith to doubt and hope to despair
It was a feral dream, an unending nightmare
A joke too cruel to tell.

Standing alone, separated from the protective presence of God
Attacked and oppressed from all sides
Abandoned to cruel fate and persecuted by hell
Painful were the stings of the northern winds
The wounds from the fall.

Whilst all these soared around me
"Adieu" said the angel with the golden voice
"Where lies the way out of these miseries?"
"Where lies the answer to all these?"
I cried to all but none in sight.

In baffling agonies of why and how
In bitter sobs of what and when
In wandering thoughts of regret, of self-pity and sorrow
Amidst the stormy billows of life searched I
Looking for the love and life once mine.

Swimming in the ocean of transgression
Afraid to go forward, more so to stand still
Night became an empty shell
Daylight a torment too fierce to bear
As hell beckoned with a pull stronger than I could repel.

Cocooned in a wall of sin, starved of love and verve
Faint of hoping, fear stricken
I tried to pray, but words failed me
Sin orphaned my soul setting a wall between me and He who fathered my spirit
Thrice I revived my claim, thrice I was beguiled.

Redemption

Rambling through the jungle of death
Where no tree grew and no life abided
There, within the bowels of mother earth
Hidden from all sights and sounds
Christ found me
He brought me forth
And set me on the garden path.

Awheel again on the cycle of life
Gliding at the Lord's sweet will
I ride through the misty clouds
To the city of the living God
The abode of true saints
There to live and stay
Never again to stray.
Jesus sets me free!

Last Note

*P*lease note, that sin drove man from the garden of the Lord to the desert, the home of wicked souls and spirits, filling his heart with the jazz from hell, eventuating his wandering in the wilderness, the wild world of sin and uncertainty; And life can only resume its former glow when man takes his place again in God's own kingdom. **Be wise, Repent and be saved!**

Chapter Two

—Love—

The Seed Of Love

There is a seed in you
There is a seed in me
The seed of love
Sown in our hearts by the Most High
Let's nurture it, water it and watch it grow
Into God's kind of love—Agape
That we may live God's kind of life—Zoë
Every durable bond is founded on love
God loves you, so o o . . . . much
And so do I!

True Love Never Dies!

Like clouds in the sky—beauty will fade
Like a day gone by—youth will pass away
Like waves on the seashore—emotions change
Like the fresh morning dew—feelings do melt away
Love is neither a mystery nor a fairy tale
But a practical reality as seen on the cross
And true love never dies!

Love Dynamics

It's the function of love to express life
The nature of life to express God
The duty of man to love God and express His life to all through love.

Love is . . . .

. . . the language of a heart attuned to God
. . . the thoughts of a mind renewed by the word
. . . the vows of a mouth controlled by the Spirit
. . . the actions of a saint walking in faith
Love is the language of heaven
An expression of life
A reflection of divinity
And true love is God in action!

God's Love Is . . . .

. . . *a* ray of hope
. . . a depth of infinite glory
. . . a gift of life
. . . a taste of paradise
God's love fills our heart
That His nature may fill this earth through us!

A New Heart

*L*ord, give me a new heart
A heart of flesh so . . . soft,
So . . . calm and so . . . fresh
A heart that glows with life
A heart of peace and joy
Of love to love all and hate none!

A New Song

Genuine love brings tears of joy
Tears lessen the grieves of the soul
Shed tears not in grief or bitterness of the soul but in love
Give a tear for all thy sorrows
A song for all thy joys
Sing the Lord a new song!

Let Our Love Grow As The Years Go By

As we move along life's track way
As our paths grow wider and seasons deepen
As folks are born and noble spirits pass away
As souls go cheerless and hearts break for want of love
Anchored on the will above
With hearts at peace with God
Let our love grow as the years go by!

Vain Love

Vain are the hundred creeds
Vain are the thousand words
Vain are the million deeds and bouquets of flowers
-if there is no love in the heart!

Love Melody

In looks and mien
In subtle words and noble deeds
In little ways so deep
And silent thoughts so wide
In loving silence, gestures and smiles
In beautiful whims and whispers
In sweet unceasing songs
Let's yodel the love that flows from the heart
The feelings that sweeten the soul!

Walk in Love

There can be no surer way
There can be no better means to overcome evil
Than to walk in love all the time.

The Angel Of Love

Like a thousand stars
-you will shine
Like the water lily
-you will bloom and blossom
Like a flower in the morning ray
-you will shine, brighter than the moon on a winter's day
Gem of creation, my love royal, my bride of divine beauty
-you are the summer rose that brightens the morning star!

Love In Little Ways

Unlike the eagle in the sky
Or the dove on the pine
But as the days gone by
Love does not grow wings and fly away
Love goes in little ways
In minutes, in hours and in days
By the little things we say or fail to say
The little things we do or fail to do
For the sake of love
Love therefore in little ways
By the little things you say or fail to say
The little things you do or fail to do
For the sake of love.

All That Matters Is Love

Purity of heart, sincerity of words and deeds is much more important than the meticulous observance of rules and laws, customs and traditions. What God desires most of all is a state of heart so pure and so right that love must ensue prima-facie.

Life Is Dynamic

here has never been and never would be a static eternal state. Life is dynamic, true life is eternal and true love endures forever.

Love Is A Weapon

ove is the weapon of all weapons, the strength of all strengths, the argument that wins all the time, the weapon that never fails.

Love is the purest, the truest and the fullest expression of life.
True love can never be faked
And true love never dies!

Chapter Three

—The Word—

God's word stretches as a parapet from the eternal past across the present into eternity. Christ has journeyed between the times. In His word He instructs and by His spirit He guides us into the age to come. Beyond space and time, well above the realms of human language and thinking, God speaks, and what He says, none can annul!

The word of God is so meaningfully structured and arranged such that one cannot add, subtract or change one verse, one word, one chapter or book without impairing on the harmony and meaning of the whole.

By the word our hearts are assayed, our deeds are graded and words are judged.

The underlining structure, forms and functions of the universe are based on the word of God—the eternal emblem, crest and seal on all creation.

Everything is controlled from the centre, the scientist calls it the nucleus but I call it the word—the centre and source of all life.

The Holy Spirit is the glue that holds the bits and pieces of the scriptures together, if we neglect Him the scriptures will fall apart.

The Christian is limited not by his physical abilities or lack of such but by his spiritual insights and revelations, his knowledge of God's word and will.

Never look down to test the ground before obeying the voice of God, if you are willing to take the risk, God will confirm His word with great testimonies.

Each verse, each chapter and book of the bible is a complete whole yet a part in a larger whole and must be interpreted inline with the larger whole—the Bible.

Never allow yourself to become a slave to the tyrants, the errand sons of hell. Use the sword of the spirit—the word of life.

The principles of God's word are of little worth, until they by practice of choice and self-will become part of our character, habit and mindset.

Just as the body without the soul is dead, the word without the Holy Spirit becomes void of power.

The entire creation is a product of the thoughts and imaginations of God lovingly spoken out into words.

The vastness, beauty, mystery and complexity of the universe can never truly be explained by science and scientists. The word of God is beyond the modern day concept of space and time continuum.

God's word far transcends the meaning we give to it.

None so wise and none so rich as the man who meets his daily needs by faith in God's word.

When we act based on God's word we receive a spiritually equivalent reward in the area of our most pressing need.

No matter the amount of storm in your life when you hear the voice of the master it calms the storms and fills you with peace.

If God's word and will, guide you, your life will be a guide for others.

When we look into the mirror of God's word we see things not the way we are but the way they truly are.

A word not spoken is never heard. A word not heard does no good. Verbalize the word in your heart and in your mouth, which is your confession. The devil may steal the thoughts in your mind but he cannot kill the word spoken out in faith.

Everything is in a state of flux, constantly changing, reforming, breaking and reforming again and again. The only constant, immoveable and unchanging, absolute and true is the **word**.

The word is the cure for all ailments, the key that unlocks every door, the solution for all life's problems.

God's word shines within the heart
-dispelling every trace of darkness
Runs through the soul
-washing away every debris of sin
Pierces the spirit, the soul and the body
-giving life to mortal beings

Grant oh Lord thy holy word
-to cloud, to rain and sun in my heart!

In the endless night of the soul
In the stillness of the heart
From the deep fountains of the spirit
His voice can be heard
One word from God is better than the babblings of a thousand men.
A word from Him is all we need!

Lord teach me delight in simple things
-your word of simple faith!

Chapter Four

Demons On Rampage

A:
Demons Everywhere!

In every generation
In all spheres of life
Assembling plants, cars and aircrafts
From the daily wash and chores
To the most intricate intellectual operations
Even on the pulpit
Demons abound!

Through sports, games and media
The ruled and the ruler
The popular and the unpopular
The wise and the fool
The rich and the poor
From the street corners
To the graveyards
Demons abound!

In every clan, town and city
Demons on the bench and bar
On the altars, thrones and kingdoms of men
On the temples and cemeteries, seashores and meadows
Up the river, over the lakes, high on the islands
Across the mountain tops
From summer fields and traces, to the corridors of power
Demons abound!

And high on the hill top
Sits the old dragon
The lity god of demons
Clothed with wild owl's feathers
Senile, cold and lonely
Twisted and pale with age
So old and so gray, dead with sorrows
Barking orders to all whose hearts are tuned to hell.

B:
Fake Pastors, False Prophets And Phony Saints:

Demons elect, false prophets and fake pastors
Masters of the game of deceit
Perverting the truth to feed their lusts
With practiced falsehood
They deceive simple souls
Using the pulpit as a hide
Willfully doomed to a lifeless existence
Theirs is the voice of a wily wolf!

Pretentious believers, wolves in sheep's clothing
Self deceived; they preach the message of hell
Laboring morning, noon and night
Digging their own graves
With increased appetite, they eat, drink and act sin
In looks and miens they mock the true saints
They, without whom the world would have long gone extinct
The road is wide that leads straight to hell!

Rogues as pastors, double fools as teachers
Collared thieves in priestly regalia
Pilfering away the substances of simple souls
Seeking recognition as true saints truly sent
With strain and stress, they wade through sin
As evidence of their sonship to the father of lies
They pervert every truth in the word to feed impious souls
Which demons have inspired them I can not tell!

Swift messengers of hell, robbers as men of God

Tutored in the classic traditions and cultures of satanic doctrines

Deaf and dumb, they only hear the jazz from hell

Fornicating with evil souls from the deep

Unwelcomed guests, they forget the way home

On the streets corners, turns and curves, they hawk their wares

Point blank they fire at the church of God

Their punishment is heaven's and not mine to say!

Ignorant scribes, Pharisees and Sadducees

Speaking for the man behind the mask

Traitors of heaven, heroes of hell

Blinded and lost they want to lead the way

With folksy charm they bewitch hungry souls

Sowing tares in God's golden fields

How this came to be their niche I cannot tell

Still, I wonder what could have led them to stray so far from life!

Guided missiles and misguided men

Toastmasters, giving vent to the voice from below

Saints in the day and monsters at night

Lost to love and life, they struggle to live

Reducing the word of life to an alimentary level

As time draws on they grow in bulk and number

Their tracks lead straight to hell

Every counterfeit gospel time will make known!

C:
The Wise In Sin;
—Godless Intellectuals;

Intellectual faggots, professors of nonsense
    With bricks as brains
        They pour out the debris of sin filled souls in poetic verses
Profoundly tearing down the knowledge of creation
The eternal emblem of the creator
With false theories of existence, deceiving simple souls
Demanding praise and pelf for demeaning their creator
Yes, you may copy but no, you can't create!

Brilliant fools as wise
Coast to coast, and pole to pole, they go
In pendulous movements of uncertainty
Swinging to and fro, looking for truth and running from truth
Looking for life yet running from life
In search of God, they resist God
Seeking for knowledge and wisdom they became double fools
Unless you repent, Pharaoh's fate shall be all yours!

Hell sent and hell bound egg-heads
With lives soon to end and brains soon to rot
They devise schemes to outsmart their creator
So unwilling to peer beyond the limiting contents of the palisade
That separates the soul from seraphic lights
That divides life from death
And parts the physical from the spiritual
Yours is an endless jogging on the spot!

Academic devils, wizards and reprobates
Lost in the conundrum of vague immensities
Entombed in the yawning blankness of nothingness
Blown about by the stellar winds
Drawn by the tug of the tides
Blinded by a cloud of scientific humbug
They swim towards self destruction
Like withered leaves, shall you fall without a sound!

Imprudent, arrogant and boastful fellows
Tenaciously, they cling to the leaves of a falling tree
Groping in blinding darkness, they claim to see
Perplexed and confused, they pretend to know all
Loitering in space and sky, as the earth sleeps below
Led and egged on by abstract intelligence
Yours is a deceptive illusion, a mirage
A chase after the wind, a journey without an end!

Vain scholars and researchers, men of alien intelligence
Daily boasting the things they know not
No; you can't make a poet of a dog
No; you can't recreate the created
You can't un-will His will, nor undo His deeds
Even you shall take your place in the dark halls of death, in the steaming depths of hell
And with a bang, shall you fall from your self defined tower
Unless you repent and be saved!

D:
Prostitutes, Sex Perverts
And Nudists

Tenants of the sin house
Members of the whorage crowd
Young, brown and blue eyed girls in scarlet shawls
Strong and fresh, crisp, curled and furled
With smiling innocence, they seduce simple souls
Standing here and there, by the road sides
Aggressively marketing their soul wares on the streets
Luring the souls of men into bondage
Truly, yours is a sorry tale!

Eagle eyed sex maniacs
Wretched souls in bond
Naked they lie, side by side, soul to soul
With demon characters from hell
Who perjure their hearts to the world of sin
Garbage cleaners, they gallivant the pathways
Looking for sin to do
Know this without a doubt
Every sin beggars the soul!

Sex perverts and nudists, tramps and bitches
With trunk-like legs of stone they run to do evil
Lost in the Sargasso sea of life
Daily piling debris on souls overloaded with sin
For a penny they submit to the devil
For a silver they pose for the crowd from below
Their world? An amorphous mass of shit
It needs no mighty prophesy to tell where they are headed!

She-men and he-women
Wild dogs, they lick the devil's wounds
Sodomites and unrepentant Ninevites
Amorous birds of prey, begging to be devoured
Duty free, they row to hell at top speed
With cargoes of sin
What a shame!
What a miserable fate!
Only Christ can put you out of this misery!

Drunkards and smokers, adulterers and fornicators
Neurotic sin addicts, spunky little imps in mini
Walking demons in bra
Whimpering to and fro looking for vain pleasures
Hear this and let it sink
The dark is littered with traps as the earth is thick with sin
Higher than the sky the clouds hang above
And more than a thousand winds that blow the word speaks
Repent and be saved!

E:
Robbers And Killers,
Kidnappers And Murderers

Demonic psychopaths, subversive agents of darkness
Hired and self styled assassins, murderers of souls
Robbers at night and fornicators in the day
Satanic night marauders, drinkers of innocent blood
They gather beneath moon-light shadows
Speaking in whispering tones
Money and lucre their arbitrating gods
Silver and gold their only reason for existence
Carrying out the enemy's charge
To kill, to steal and destroy.

Cloned devils, miserable thieves and killers
Kidnappers of destiny and robbers of life
Errant sons of Satan, fugitives of time
Hell prisoners on parole
Abbevillean breeds
With wolfish appetite, they devour their prey
To satisfy mad dream desires
Though their sins fill a sea
They grief not for what they've done
But straight in they dive to drown!

Cannibalized souls
Devil sent rascals from beneath
Evil maniacs, roving dogs on prowl
With loads of guilt they labour along
Running from life and hastening to hell
Floating on a sea of iniquity
As the stars float across the night sky
One day you shall wake up to see the vainness of your life
The emptiness of your existence
The meaninglessness of a life without God!

Scums of the earth, serial killers and avowed robbers
With smiling calm they slay their victims
Wasting lives at will
Intoxicated with blood as wine
Spurred on by the wages of sin
What a labor of hate!
What a strange fate!
What a forte to bear!
Tell me, what manner of beast are you?
Why take a life if you can't give one?

Hooded masquerades and rapists

Hijackers, bombers and terrorists

Looting, killing and maiming innocent lives

Freely shedding blood on whim

Pouring oil on the fire that ravage their souls

The sovereign Lord sees all

"The sinner will never go unpunished" He says

In the great silence of the grave

There would be no chance of repentance

Your chance to live is here and the hour to love is now!

Mafia gangsters and sadists, rebel leaders and followers

Arsonists and militants, wayward souls in bondage

Political thugs and hoodlums, religious soreheads

This day could be your last; this hour could be your best

If only you could pause a while, stop a bit

To meditate on the true meaning of life

As the closing of a book, your life draws to an end

But you can still repent and live even now

Life is ahead of you, go for it, forsake evil and embrace life

Yes, you can, you truly can, if you dare!

F:
Idol worshippers, Cultists and Ritualists, Witches and Wizards, Voodoo Priests, Kings And Queens

Religious castaways, members of the satanic chaplaincy
Worshipers of pagan gods
Dirty as a pig, they refuse to be washed
Wan and thirsty, abject and beggarly
They reject the bread and river of life
Leprotic and lame, sick and dying
They wobble to hell with great zests
Slaving for hell and relishing in the internal conflicts
And contradictions of their sin filled souls
What a strange faith!

Men of vain superstitions and heathen philosophy
Custodians of traditions, of customs and cultures of hell
Their hearts became shrines for the worship of worthless idols
In their hearts, their sins sit
In their souls they rest
Deeper than the sea
Higher than the clouds
Yet, at the slightest scent of sin
Incited by the murmurs of hell
They rush to make sacrifices as demons scream for blood!

Vampires and vagabonds
Werewolves and scarecrows
Smiling owls and dandy demons
Red robbed, hooded priests and ministers of hate
Sworn enemies of the living one, obligate outlaws
Rioting to protest divine injunctions
Compulsive law breakers, resisting the laws of life
Religious yoyos, worshipping dummy gods
Mummified souls in martial guise
These are folks in conscious grip of hell!

Nimrods of the Dark Age,
Ambassadors of Satanic kingdoms
Occultists and ritualists, witches and wizards
Eaters of flesh and drinkers of blood
Mystic and psychic ministers of death
Execrable fools, philosophical satanics
Down the pit they mock those on high
In quickened steps they rush to pagan temples
To receive instructions from the evil one
Hell is a long, long night!

Denizens of the evil forest

Tenants of satanic hermitage

Religious pretenders, jesters and jokers

Ill mannered comedians

Playing sports with the creator's will

In slow procession they match, straight on to hell

To be churned into spots and bits

Of particles, of dust, of grain and air

This is the time to wail and weep

To yell for help and be saved!

Voodoo kings, herbal gods and native priests

Stargazers and astral travelers

Migrant sons of the air

By deeds and vows, they choreograph the symphony of hell

Animated by the jazz from the deep

Trapped in the illusions of false rewards

They follow the speeding flood to the drains

Yours is an eerie comedy

A cruel joke, a psychic release

Unless you repent hell shall be all yours to dwell!

G:
Wicked Rulers, Corrupt Politicians, Officers And Officials

Evil rulers, Machiavellian syndicates

Human predators and terminators

Dictators and despots, feudal lords and vassals

Vaunting tyrants, depraved souls as leaders

Wayward wanderers of a sinking earth

Trapped in the illusions of false achievements

Walking through the dark corridors of mortal power

Swollen in the celebratory gaiety of ill gotten riches

Hell is an unending night of woes and horror!

Ornamental legends of the dooms stage

Patrons of a dying world

Sailors in a floating ship

Hopeless thieves and robbers as rulers

Struggling in vain to find peace

In a world at war with self

Striving for love in a theatre of war

Looking for light in a sin field

Seeking for help from the helpless one.

Bribe givers, takers and bearers
Animal brutes, torturers and bullies
Uniformed charlatans and bandits on the highways
Licensed thieves and killers in starched clothes
Captives of the damned, they eat to damn their souls
With heavy boots and stuffy clothes they match on to hell
As time unwinds her coils
Every due would be paid and every debt settled
Every word would be tried, every deed judged, damned or
justified!

Elite scholars, brilliant lawyers of lies, doctors of death
Men of fraud and avarice, managers of stolen estates
Looters of the common wealth
Worshippers of the mammon god
Contractors of public assets
Sucking dry the poor
Living at the expense of wretched souls
Mark not time by the way the wind blows
Your time would soon be up!

Desperate power seekers

Political thieves in flowing gowns

Election riggers in designer's wears

Strange bed fellows of mermaids

With songs and praises they worship worldly power

Exchanging precious souls for powers that do not last

By words and deeds they pledge allegiance to the cursed one

Those who approve the eloquence of sin

Shall receive the mountain fall, the wages thereof!

Messianic pharaohs, sinners in royal garbs

Medaled chiefs, kings and queens, sit-tight despots

Aristocratic fiends, representatives of the dark world

Patriots of satanic kingdoms, evil men as gods

Suffering from power induced lunacy

As hell becomes your birthday present

And Hades your doomsday gift

What would be said in your praise?

Tell me 'what would be your final story when the day is done and the night is come?

Last Note:

*P*ity you may say, horrible I should add, but these and more are the different shades, shapes and sizes of demonic characters on rampage; and prostrate before the luciferian horde, they beg to do more while their cannibal master watches, stretches himself, sighs a belch and yawns for more; and there would yet be a cosmic outbursts of demon spirits on this planet as time draws to an end, beware!

Chapter Five

Wisdom For The Wise

Life is not lived in heavy currents, in big speeches and actions; Life is lived in seconds, in minutes, in hours, day by day moment by moment by the little things we do or fail to do, the little things we say or fail to say for the sake of God and man. Every second, every minute and every hour of your life matters to your destiny. **Be wise**!

Faith is not for mockers, love is not a pretence; in thoughts, in words and deeds, we make a choice for life. **Be wise**!

Knowledge is infinite, wisdom is without an end and truth is immortal; in the wilderness of life we wander still, he who abhors the truth lives a false life; he who rejects the shepherd's guide goes astray. **Be wise**!

This day could just be your best day ever, this hour could just be your finest; **Be wise**; live it to the fullest, to the glory of He who made you!

A tree they say can not make a forest but a seed can. **Be wise**; sow a seed when in need!

Outside purpose life is a burden, a load, a big weight, an endless jogging on the spot. **Be wise!**

Yesterday is gone, tomorrow is an illusion. All you have is today; the best hour to live is now; the best time to start is now procrastination is a thief. **Be ware!**

The whole duty of the devil is to disqualify you from the life after here. Your whole duty should be to qualify for the life after here. **Be wise**!

Darkness is a state of lifelessness, a sin field, the absence of God. **Be wise**; live in the light of God's word!

Sin when germed in the soul brings death to the body. **Be wise**; flee from sin!

Hell is a place for fools. **Be wise**; don't play the fool!

The Christian does not need a wind vane or a weatherman to know which way the wind blows. Your guide is within!
Be wise!

You don't sit or walk with a vision; you run with a vision as far and as fast as you can. **Be wise!**

God has not just given you a niche, a purpose to fulfill but has also fitted, equipped and empowered you for it. **Be wise** go for it while you can!

One act of obedience can cause an explosion of miracles in your life. **Be wise**; obey that voice of His!

The plane truth, the universal message is that life on its own means nothing without God, but a mere sound, sheer activity, a dance, a rite, a show, an endless jogging on the spot. **Be wise**; life is real because God is real!

An idle mind is crude, unrefined, untrained and unproductive. **Be wise**! Get your mind busy!

Every man is either more or less than what his first appearance suggests. Look beyond the screen; see beyond the words and façade, there is something more. **Be wise!**

Never allow the opinion of men to form the fulcrum of your life; be guided by the word and be led by the spirit. **Be wise!**

Knowledge, wisdom and anointing increase and expand with use. Ask for more by using that which you already have**. Be wise!**

The present is a reflection of what has been, a starting point for what would be. **Be wise!** your future starts now!

Whatever the devil says, whatever he suggests or gives, you have the right and the ability to accept or reject. **Be wise**! Say no to the devil!

Teach Me To Be Wise

Lord, teach me to be wise!
To pray when I should and sing when I'm glad
To seek for direction when I'm lost and ask questions when I do not know
To mourn with those who mourn
And rejoice with them that rejoice
To dance and laugh when I ought and cry when I must
To walk in the spirit and live by faith
Lord, teach me to be wise!

To continue to abide by your laws and precepts
To know and understand thy times and seasons
To embrace the glory that warms my heart
To live by the mercy of your means
To express your life young and fresh
To be deaf to the voice from hell
And dumb to tell crooked lies
To see thy light where no sun shines
The river of life where no stream runs
To drink from the brook that never dries
Oh' teach me to be wise indeed!

To forget the days of slavery
And fix my eyes on the things above
The glory that awaits my soul
For wisdom is as priceless as gold
As strong as death
As rich as life
Lord, teach me to be wise in thee!

Yesterday is gone, today is going and tomorrow would soon be here; few hours yet before the dawn, few miles to the end of age; as we approach the finishing line, time would be prompt to end. What would you give as a ransom for your soul? **Be wise!**

Chapter Six

Nuggets Of Truth

When faith is all that you say and love all that you do, life would be all that you have.

Neither life nor death is an act of accident; we were all born to live, yet every man dies of his own making, one way or the other.

There is an eternal being of supreme intelligence, of infinite wisdom and power who keeps this creation together with divine precision.

Your heart is your world and your world is in your heart.

Thinking is life in silent motion; if you think right you'll act right, if you think wrong you'll act wrong.

They may change in form, they may change in size, shape or content, but life's problems never go away, they only shift base and none but he who spoke things into being can speak them out of existence.

Dreams, visions, hopes and desires are necessary to keep life going, for without vision the people perish.

Your present life is a seed, don't eat it, sow it for an inheritance hereafter.

Roses they say do not rustle in the wind and you are more than a rose.

The present is a reflection of what has been, a picture of what would be.

By self will, by the force of men, angels or nature, we are somehow made submissive to a higher authority and this is without an option or a choice.

The world within rules the world without as the faith within cancels the fear without.

Man does not just answer for his actions but also for his inactions.

Everything is controlled from the centre and every centre is controlled by a higher centre as every life is controlled by a higher form of life.

Our illusions of safety and justice, of love and peace in a world of sin must for our own sakes be shattered in line with divine principles of sowing and reaping.

In a variety of ways man has sinned and stills sins, but the greatest sin amongst men today is the rejection of the truth and the commonest sin amongst Christians today is the sin of omission, in thoughts, words and deeds.

As we sow we reap, not just according to divine principles but according to divine times and seasons.

One of the greatest lessons of life is to know one's strengths and weaknesses, to maximize the former and minimize the latter.

Time will bring to birth the wisdom of God, His purpose in creation and the reasons for this existence.

In one way or the other every man is born a genius but only a few become one; you can be one of the few if you dare.

The spiritual endowments compliment the natural, yet the latter is eternally useless without the former.

The physical synergizes with the spiritual to make every man a complete whole.

Every mind is a gold mine waiting to be mined.

The spiritual and natural endowments combine with the anointing to make every believer a champion in his field or calling.

Every God-given dream or assignment is achievable with what you have at any point in time.

No man is truly hopeless who has a functionally renewed mind.

Every question has an answer and every problem a solution somewhere; if you ask long enough you will have an answer, if you seek long enough you will find a solution.

Every principle is controlled by a higher principle and every law by a higher law; in the final analysis everything is controlled from above.

Every tide comes with currents of problems and opportunities for us to choose from.

Your eternal future is determined by the little things you do or fail to do, the little things you say or fail to say while here on earth.

There is no dead end in life; Search for the hidden way, that little track way until you find it. **Believe me, there is always a way!**

Within every problem or crisis in life is an opportunity to make your dreams come true.

God in all His acts deals with what matters most.

Every dream needs a definite plan, strength and sense of purpose to come true.

Every man needs the protection of God's word against his own weaknesses.

God does not just count in life, He is the only one that truly counts and without Him nothing else counts.

God is the silent but active partner in all business of life. He decides the final outcome, the ultimate fate of every soul.

Your mind is a great mine to mine at will.

The price of life must be paid here or hereafter. **Every thing in life has a price tag.**

Christians must necessarily run in opposite direction to the rest of the world.

Man does not fully know what he is capable of doing until he is challenged and dared; you can be great if you dare!

Conquer your fears and conquer your world.

The cares and problems of this world are vague, like the wind upon the roses, the wind passes and the roses are brighter.

Why mind the thorns when you can pick the roses?

Let you faith rise above your fears and your dreams will rise above your nightmares.

In spite of the difficulties, failures and frustrations of the moment, you can still dream big dreams and your dreams can yet come true.

In life every end necessarily signifies a beginning somewhere and every beginning an end somewhere else.

Every problem in life comes with an opportunity to make you a better person.

No man dies a success who had lived outside God's will.

Every talent, gift or skill comes as a seed to be trained and nurtured through use.

You are like a dream, a promise coming true, refuse to be aborted, don't give up your dreams; they are your seeds for greatness.

The devil's best shot is not enough to stop you, keep going!

Make a habit of maximizing your potentials and moments of opportunities, they might never come again.

At each point and at all times as the opportunities come your way give life your best shot. Do your best with what you have at any point in time.

Every trying time reveals a strength or a weakness in you.

Your present situation is the truest reflection of your past choices.

Even amidst quarrels and differences let not your heart shift from the truth.

True, Christians may differ and at times quarrel over issues of doctrines and behaviours, but one purpose unites us all "to preach Christ and the cross to every creature".

Never surrender yourself to the will, plans and purposes of the devil, whatever the cost and agony may be.

Every law is subject to a higher law and every life to a higher form of life.

At whatever cost, whatever be the physical pain, you must conquer the enemy of your soul, the cost may be great but the reward is greater and eternal.

Every heaven conscious Christian must have zero tolerance for sin.

Nothing can stop a man whose focus is on God and nothing can help a man whose focus is on man.

It is vital for men to focus diligently, wisely and prayerfully on the sole object of their life—God's purpose for them.

Men are naturally ordained, anointed and empowered for a singular purpose on earth; every other vocation is a distraction.

The power-releasing-contact-point lies in your ability as a Christian to connect heaven to your situations here on earth
this is called—faith.

Freedom in whatever guise is a function of knowledge. Every ignorant man is in bondage.

Every one born into this world must choose one of two roads in life; the broad and crowded road that leads to hell or the straight and narrow one that leads to heaven.

That which is popular, pressing and pleasant before men may command no eternal rewards and hence no divine backing.

Too often we fail, so ruefully and woefully to recognize and utilize our inner abilities, powers and strengths in times of needs, problems or crisis.

To love life and run from life is a contradiction found only in man.

The power of choice has been freely given to all; the exercise of it is entirely a matter of choice.

Life and death are two opposite extremes without a mid point, likewise, sin and righteousness, love and hate, heaven and hell, and we can only make a choice for one at a time.

It pays to do things the beautiful way, God's own way. Get it right the first time, it costs less and pays more.

This may be painful but true, for a true believer to leave this earth is no loss but gain.

Times' orders none can annul!

Only God can see the man behind the mask, the soul beyond the face, the heart beneath the flesh.

Those whose niche it is to pervert the truth shall peace elude.

Reject the truth, refute and resist it, the truth it remains. Nothing can change the unchangeable and truth is unchangeable.

Life in its truest and most divine state is an expression of God, an extension of divinity.

Success in life rests squarely on meeting and overcoming obstacles and challenges that litter the paths of life.

God never wastes anything; He renews everything including our mortal bodies.

Nothing in the entire universe is a product of chance; every thing is a product of deliberate choice and will.

None so blind as the man who can not see God in His creation.

Life is free but we live at will.

Our strength as a church lies in the strengths of each member of the church.

Your thoughts, words and actions reflect your faith.

Every failure in life presents an opportunity to do better.

Your most valued and most important assets, your greatest gifts and talents are often but necessarily hidden, invisible and intangible.

Destiny is an eternal thing, it goes beyond here, it continues hereafter; if you don't live now you might never live again.

Every believer is differently anointed for a different purpose.

We Christians are in a spiritual warfare and the only guarantee we have for victory is that we hear and obey the master's voice and fight according to His instructions.

Life was not created but given and the gift of life comes with the manual for life—the bible.

Your purpose is your identity in life.

There is nothing like the all time best because the best is yet to come.

Every part and bit of your life fits to form the whole and real you.

There is no situation in this life that is truly final, no; not even death.

These two define your height in life, your position and what you do with it.

There would always be easier and better ways of doing things.

To be great in life learn to do little things in great ways.

No matter how good you are; learn this simple truth; the world would be a horrible place if all men were like you.

In moments of prayer, praise or worship our heart's intents speak louder than our mouth.

Our lives as Christians are like a mirror to reflect God to the world.

Nothing is as bad as it looks if God's presence can be felt.

God will always tell us what to do but whether we do them or not is our choice.

Purpose is not about self, not about money, power or fame; your role within a larger role, your function within a larger function, your part within a larger part, that's your purpose.

Chapter Seven

Warning Notes

. . . . Beware . . . .

*I*f we could but have a passing glimpse, a glancing view of the hearts of men, I shrink at what would be found!
Beware!

Knowledge is infinite, wisdom is without an end, but truth is immortal, and he who abhors the truth rejects his own life.
Beware!

God's universal time has already been set, His plans have been settled before time; and none can stop His hand at work.
Within us all, deep in the centre of our being, we can hear the ticks of God's clock; at the zero hour, we, the rapturable saints would know, we need no man to tell us when.
Beware!

The devil does not come with the heavy streams and currents of life. The devil comes in little ways and subtle manners, by the little things we see, the little things we hear, the little things we think, speak or do; this is the way of the evil one.
Beware!

Never try to undo that which God has done, never try to unsay that which God has said and never try to falsify the word of God, for all who believe in lying vanities forsake their mercy.
Beware!

There are no idle demons and there are no idle angels, but idle Christians, daily falling prey to the tricks of busy demons.
Beware!

Every sin has a price tag.
Beware!

Know this and don't ever forget, whoever you are, wherever you are and whatever you are doing, saying or thinking; there is always an unseen presence, watching and recording for eternal judgment and condemnation or commendation and reward.
Beware!

It is God that holds the bits and pieces of our lives together, if we neglect Him our lives fall apart.
Beware!

Every sin debits the soul.
Beware!

There is no greater truth than this "that life is from God", and no greater lie than this "that life is a product of chance."
Beware!

Every evil cause is followed by an effect which becomes increasingly unpleasant as time rolls by and every good deed is followed by an effect which becomes increasingly better as time rolls by.

Beware!

Destiny is an infinite thing, yet within a moment in a layer of time one's destiny can be destroyed.

Beware!

Those whose aim is to destroy the gospel shall by same be destroyed, and all who rejects life shall in death abide.

Beware!

Every child knows his father except them that have gone astray; he who rejects the creation story falsifies his own existence.

Beware!

In God's glorious kingdom, no trace of sin shall abide; every sin is either forgiven or punished.

Beware!

A denial of truth is an acceptance of falsehood, a denial of good is an acceptance of evil, and a denial of life is an acceptance of death, a denial of Christ is an acceptance of Satan.

Beware!

Those who approve the eloquence of sin shall receive the mountain fall, the wages thereof.

Beware!

The road to heaven runs straight and narrow, the road to hell wide and crooked.

Beware!

Sin beggars the soul.
Beware!

Sin in whatever form, shape or size has a downward pull on the soul.
Beware!

Each time a man sins something in him dies.
Beware!

Every man must either be born again or die again. We are born again to live again after here.
Beware!

If you listen long enough, you'll hear a voice where no one speaks and if you look long enough, you'll see a mountain where a molehill does not exist.
Beware!

Purpose is like hunger until it is satisfied nothing else satisfies.
Beware!

No one man sees things the way they truly are, we see things the way we are.
Beware!

Christianity is not a part time job, but a lifestyle, half measures and short cuts are not allowed.
Beware!

The Running Tide

The rains fall, and the sun shines
The wind blows and the oceans surge hot and fierce
As time races by along life's rocky way
The moon and the stars, even the heavens above
None can His word disobey
Every man must one day answer the call of the running tide
You never can tell when life would be gone.
Beware!

It's the mind that hears and not the ears
It's the mind that sees and not the eyes
It's the mind that speaks and not the mouth
The senses are mere instruments of sin or righteousness.
Beware!

Chapter Eight

Life Is Like A Journey

Life is like a journey; your future starts just where you are right now.

In the great journey of life there is no speed limit, you go as far as you can and as fast as your abilities allow.

In the journey of life every man starts from where he left off. Forget what has been, you can start all over again just from where you are now.

Life is like a journey and the higher you go in life the greater you should appreciate the giver of life.

In the journey of life every man is on his own lane traveling at his own speed.

Life is like a journey and God takes you as far and as long as you are willing to go with him.

In the journey of life the shortest distance between two points is a straight line but the shortest distance between two persons is love.

Life is like a journey all physical yet all spiritual; don't neglect one for the other.

Life is like a journey; to stay on course stick to your guide.

In the journey of life looking back drags you back and slows down your speed; focus on your future and you won't see your past.

In the journey of life you can never get ahead of any man because you are on your own lane traveling at your own speed.

The journey of life has no bus-stops; keep going until you get to your destination.

Life is like a journey; your are today where your past choices have brought you and you would be tomorrow where your present choices take.

Life is like a journey; our thoughts, words and actions often travel in the direction of our beliefs.

Life is like journey; we define our path in life, we create our world by the little things we think, the little things we say and the little things we do.

Life is like a journey; and the man who runs is not faster than the man who walks, our speed in life should be a reflection of our destination in life.

Life is like a journey; the devil's aim is to change the course and destination if we allow him; stay on course and your destiny is assured.

Life is like a journey; and God can lengthen or shorten it to suit His eternal plans for us.

In the journey of life no true Christian dies on the way but at times God ferries us across the bumps and turbulences with divine precision.

In the journey of life, he who travels with Christ never dies; yes, we can ascend but we do not die, we cannot die!

Life is like a journey; and the unseen presence is always there, protecting, guiding and leading us along life's track way.

In the journey of life there can be no meaningful movement outside Christ.

Life is like a journey; and the faster we go without Christ the more dangerous the journey becomes.

In the journey of life speed is not as important as focus, proper planning and direction.

Life is like a journey; and sin, a great distraction that causes our vehicle to stutter, to breakdown, stop and abort the journey; flee from sin!

Life is like a journey; with Christ we ride on the crest to heaven's gate into God's warm embrace, without Him we crash into hell.

Life is like a journey; in all situations keep moving, don't stop until you hear the welcome songs from above.

Life is like a journey; eternal life is life's crowning glory, and hell life's final punishment.

In the journey of life the man who is crawling is better than the man who is running but in the wrong direction.

In the journey of life some are passengers and some drivers in the vehicle of life.

Life is like a journey and the reward for a truly successful life is eternity with God.

Life is like a journey; the worth of your life is what you give to life. **Give to life your very best!**

Life is like a journey; to keep living is to keep moving, to stop is to die. Don't die on the way, keep moving!

Life is like a journey; heaven would not be a surprise to those who made it, likewise hell.

Life is like a journey that begins with birth and ends with death, every life is defined betwixt these two times.

Life is like a journey and the greatest fear in the journey of life is the fear of the unknown. Where do you go from here?
Where would you spend eternity?

Every journey must one day come to an end and one day the journey of life would come to a final stop; what would be your story at the end of time?

Life is like a journey, you never can say when, how and where it will end; **Be ready at all time!**

Chapter Nine

Poems And Rhymes

Telling My Bride I'm Coming soon!

I need a bride
A friend to show my love and share my glory
One who can smile and sing
A princess of love to love
A heroine of faultless heart
Made in divine artistry
A perfection of motherhood
A maiden bride to call mine
Tell my bride I'm coming soon!

I need a bride
A friend that understands my gestures, smiles and silence
My beautiful bride in golden array
My only choice amongst the crowd
A saint in thoughts, words and deeds
Free from stains, spots and wrinkles
One to love and wed
A queen befitting the throne above
Tell my bride I'm coming soon!

A bride kind and gentle, true and just
Real in faith and strong in love
Clothed in righteousness, symboled in sainthood
My bride for whom I died
Tell my bride I coming soon
And if somehow I delay
Wait for me and ask not what stayed me
For all I do is for your good and to the father's glory
Tell my bride I coming soon!

My Pledge

I vow to thee—Father God
The service of my love
The praise of my lips
And the worship of my heart

I vow to thee—Brother Christ
All worldly things to denounce
All earthly wealth to forgo
All knowledge and wisdom to unlearn for the crown above

I vow to thee-Spirit Friend
To listen and obey, every instruction and leading
To follow thee along the straight and narrow path
To the kingdom above

I pledge to thee—Father, Son and Spirit
To unspeak every wrong word
To undo every wrong deed
To live by that faith that stands all tests

To light thy candle in my heart
And curse the darkness of the soul
To live for thee every day of my life
This is my pledge, so help me God!

His Grace Is Amazing

Tests and trials may come
Fears may assail
Visions may dim and dreams die
Yet in His word we have faith and hope
A promise to find, the courage to bear and the life to live
Therein we find the grace to laugh, to sing and smile
The strength to stand and endure
As God uses every obstacle
And every set back along life's rocky way
To set us on a higher plane
And bring us nearer home
Indeed this grace is amazing!

Heaven Is My Home

Hell is a place for those who were born to live
Who should have lived
-but refused to live
Those who were born to be sons
-but lived as slaves
Men who were made to be giants
To fly higher than the eagle
-but crawled all their days
Those born to be saints
-but lived as devils
Hell is theirs and not mine to dwell
-heaven is my home!

A Heart Cry

Lord, take me to the mountain top
Above the waves and storms of life
Beyond my innermost fears
Above the wiles of the devil
Beyond the shadows of death
To grace the stars of God
To hear the heavenly songs of praise
Take me Lord to the kingdom above
Where no sin bears, there to live and stay
Never again to stray!

The Hungry Soul

Deep, within the inner recesses of the soul
There, in the centre of the mortal being
Lies a void, like a gulf
Waiting to be filled
Hungry for satisfaction and fulfillment
Yet nothing, absolutely nothing
But an acceptance of God's will satisfies a hungry soul!.

Sin

Sin—an act of admission, omission or permission
A thought entertained, spoken or not
A word said or unsaid
A restraint to do right
An urge to do ill
In subtle ways and manners, we all sin
By the little things we do or fail to do
The little things we say or fail to say
Sin—a promise broken
A trust betrayed, His grace beguiled
Our faith compromised and a destiny destroyed
More than a cancer sin kills
Get rid of sin before it gets rid of you!

Beyond The Grave

Beyond the night is the dawn
Beyond the rains the sun
Beyond the desert is the garden
Beyond the seas, the promise land
Beyond the cross is the crown of life
Beyond death is the life Christ gives
And beyond the grave is the city of God
The home of righteous souls!

Shadows Of The Real

The best of riches, of knowledge and wisdom
The best of thoughts, of words and deeds
The best of talents, of beauty and gold
All that we can see
All that we can hear, feel or touch here on earth
Are nothing but shadows of the real!

Echoes From Above

Somewhere, somehow, down the heart of every man
Within the deep waters of the soul
Beyond emotions, logics and reasons
Resides the human spirit
From which flow the issues of life
Whence we hear the voice from within
The echoes from above!

The Brighter Side Of Life

The tide recedes
-but leaves behind bright seashells on the shore
The sun goes down
-but gentle warmth lingers on on the land
The music stops
-yet it echoes on in sweet refrains
For every experience that passes something beautiful remains!

He Set Me Free

Rambling through the jungle of death
Swimming through the deep-sea of sin
Where no tree grows and no life abides
Down, within the bowels of mother earth
Hidden from all sights and sounds
He brought me forth
And set me on the garden path
Awheel again on the cycle of life
I ride through the misty clouds
To the city of God
The lands of golden streets and summer fields
The home of righteous soul
There, to live and be
Never again to stray
Jesus set me free!

Your Life As A Seed

Take care of the fundamentals
-and the incidentals will take care of themselves
Take care of the seconds
-and the minutes will take care of themselves
Take care of the minutes
-and the hours will take care of themselves
Take care of the hours
-and the days will take care of themselves
Take care of the days
-and the months will take care of themselves
Take care of the months
-and the years will take care of themselves
Take care of the years
-and life will take care of itself
Take care of your life
-and eternity will take care of itself
Every second of every minute of every hour of every day of your life is a race to run
Every year a spot in eternity
The past determines the present
The present determines the future
Your present life on earth determines your future in eternity
Your time here is your capital to invest
Your seed to sow for an inheritance hereafter
Don't squander it.
Be wise!

I Need Time

I need time, time to get away from this madness
Time to go blank and recharge myself
To seek my God and find the centre again
I need time, time to get away from the crowd
To walk the seaside, to watch the falling waves
And feel the rushing winds
To tour the valleys and behold the freezing snows
Time to think my thoughts and dream my dreams
Time to play, to dance and merry
To laugh and sing my songs

Dear Lord, I need more time
To study and meditate upon your word
To bask in your love and float in your grace
To pray and do your biddings
To read and write beautiful poems of the love from above
Yes, I need time, time beyond time
To love, to praise, to worship and adore
To sing your grace and intone your wonders
I need time, timeless time, time eternal
To do your will in an endless life of bliss.

The Voice Within

Deep, down the human heart
There, within the fountains of the spirit
Lies the answer to all questions
That could arise in the course of life's journey
If only we can pause a while, stop a bit
To listen, to hear and obey
The voice within—the Spirit of truth!

There Is A Mission To Your Life

There is a purpose and a reason for every second of every minute of
every day
There is a purpose and a reason to the sun, the moon and the stars
There is a purpose and a reason to every plant and animal
To all events and seasons of life
There is a mission to every living soul or creature
The reason for its creation
The why of its existence
The what of its being
And there is a purpose, a reason, a mission for your life
Find It!

Golden Thoughts

One bright summer morning
Walking through a winding wooded path
Ferns unfurled and squirrels scolded
Sat I upon a rock seat
Beside a crystal stream, my back against the taper's tree
Lost in silent but golden thoughts unspoken
Thoughts of thanks expressed in songs
Thoughts of faith expressed in hope and courage
Thoughts of love, of bliss and beauty of the kingdom above
Expressed in poetic rhymes, verses and quotes
My thoughts are my heart felt love for God and His saints
What do you think about?

The Heart Diary

In the heart of every man
Within the deep recesses of all mortal soul
Is an eternal diary
Wherein are written all he has done or failed to do
All he has said or failed to say
Therein lies the story of his life
What would be your eternal story?
What would you tell your maker?
One soul is worth all the treasures the world can give
And one word, one just deed is a treasure to your soul!

Who Can Save The Dead

No power on earth can a dead soul awaken
None can rouse him from the dead
Call him back to life
Breathe on him again the breath of life
Whom God has deemed eternally dead
Live now while you can, as much as you care
For none can save the dead!

The Face Behind The Wall

Every act leaves a trace
Every word leaves an echo
Every thought makes us better, wiser or worse
Every scene brings memories
There is always a face behind the wall
An unseen eye beyond the scene!
Be ware!

Life Is Not By Chance

The wandering stars do not mock
The running tides do not guile
Life is not a rite, not a dance and not a guise
The origin of life no mortal can date
The end of time none can foretell
For deeper than sense is the wisdom from above
Higher than intellectual reach, the knowledge of God
It wounds my soul and grieves my heart to utter what would be the lot of men lost
in the ocean of mortal life
Believe not the lying mouths of science and philosophy
Regard not the singing voices of false prophets
Shouting aloud from the silence of the grave
Heed the voice from above
Life is not by chance!

Christ Makes the Difference

That Christ came down from heaven
-is no big deal
That He lived a good and godly life and wrought great miracles
-is not the issue
But that He came, He lived, was crucified, died and rose again, all for mankind
-makes all the difference!

Watch And Pray

It is worthwhile for us to watch and pray
When the day is born and the sun is so low in the sky
Before we greet the morning ray or hallo the next door neighbor
For the enemy is out there, lurking around the streets seeking whom to devour

It is worthwhile for us to watch and pray
When the day is far spent and the sun is so high in the sky
Before we lay down to sleep or bid the day the final bye
For he is the god of darkness

For we have an enemy
Who never stops fighting
Though he's down
Never will stop tempting human souls

He has a way, he has an aim, he has his agents
Beware of them all
Heed the master's commands
Watch and pray!

The Unwilling Captive

In more ways than one
Directly or indirectly, consciously or not
Every man is a prisoner
Of his own fame, his own wealth, knowledge or beliefs
So much so that he becomes an unwilling captive
Of what he owns, what he knows or believes
As he looses his personality, his essence
In things less than shadows of the real
What would you give as a ransom for your soul?

The Devil Can Not Stop Me

When the night is done
Comes a lightening ray from above
God's symbol of a glorious dawn
And when this piece of clay is done
My spirit shall ascend to be with Him
There to live, never again to stray
The devil can't stop me!

All That Is Mine For All That Could Be Mine

One bright summer day
Just before the fall of the evening tide
Took I a walk along a garden path
Amid the growing grass, beneath a citrus tree
There I sat beside a rose
Alone amongst the wise
I niched my thoughts on things that have been
All that is and those to come
I thought of many souls
Who now are not, but were or soon would be
Of all that were theirs or soon would be
But now belong to others to use as willed
Yet, on and on, men go,
To and fro, they lope across the darkening globe
Acquiring wealth and learning more and more
Neglecting their hungry souls
As the day wore on
The clouds grew grey and sang with a thundering sound
As rain filtered down the fruit tree
I journeyed home with one thought in mind
To give all that is mine for all that could be mine

Life As A Mirage

Two people rarely say the same thing
Two people rarely see the same thing
Two people rarely hear the same thing
Two people rarely feel the same way
For things are rarely what they appear to be

Destiny As A Choice!

Somehow, somewhere we all are
Actors and observers in the events of life
At times we can help
At other times we cannot
At times we are on the stage
At other times part of the watching audience
At times we are on the field of play
At other times with the spectating crowd
At times we dance and sing victory songs
At other times we grieve for failures
At times we are victims
At other times true villains
But this much I know
Destiny is by choice as much as by fate
Sons we all are, yet I choose to be one
Fated to live, I choose to live
Your destiny is truly your choice!

A Song From Above

The Lord shall give you a song
A song of love from above
A song like a lullaby
To soothe aching nerves
A balm, to heal wounded hearts and comfort lonely souls
A cradle sound from on high
An echo from His heart
To dispel the worries of yesterday
To sing the joy of this day and the glory to come
Treble, tenor and bass in life eternal
The good Lord will give you a song!

He's Made All Things New

From doubts and uncertainties
-I've learned to trust
From hate and bitterness
-I've learned to love and cherish
From deaths and sorrows
-I've learned to live and bear
Beyond tests, trials and temptations
-I've learned to hope and pray
Happy days are meant to be mine again
He's made all things new!

Live In little Ways

God does not express Himself once in a day, twice in a month or trice in a year

God expresses His love, His grace and mercies for us

In moments, in seconds of every minute of every day

By the little things He says or fails to say

The little things He does or fails to do

All for our good

Let us therefore express His love and extend His grace to all

By the little things we say or fail to say

The little things we do or fail do

For the sake of God and for the good of all

Resist The Stranger's Goods

The devil cannot give health, wealth or fame
-for he hasn't any
The devil cannot give wisdom or knowledge
-for he has perverted all true knowledge and wisdom
The devil cannot give love or care
-for his heart is hate filled
The devil can neither give faith, nor hope
-for his case is a hopeless one
The devil cannot give life
-for his, is a dead soul
All the devil has are stolen goods
Each time a man receives from him
He looses more in return
As he pays from his own soul
Be wise resist the stranger's goods!

We are Because He Is

That the devil is, is not mine to mind
That he schemes, tricks and tempts, is not in doubt
That men would hate and persecute, is well known to me
That hell is real is none of mine to fear
But that God is, is my trust and joy
That His word is true, is my faith unfailing
That heaven is real, is my hope fulfilling
That I live, is all the proof I need that God is
For we are because He is!

The Bridge Of Life

Between this phase and eternity
-there is a gulf and a bridge
Between this life and death
-there is a gulf and a bridge
Between hell and heaven
-there is a gulf and a bridge
Between God and man
-there is a gulf and a bridge
Jesus is the bridge of life!

This Day Is Not Mine

Whether we are old, middle aged or young
Whether we are wise or foolish, rich or poor
Whether we are strong or weak, learned or not
None of us boldly can say
-this day is mine
Every minute of every day of every year of our lives
Belongs to Him who made us
To be used, not as a fad but as He directs
This day is not mine!

The Gift Of A New Day

The moon has taken a rest
The stars all in rem
As the sun breaks forth
From the eastern sphere
The birds sing and praise
The lilies and roses silently drink the morning dew
The trees clap and dance
To the tunes of gentle winds
Heralding the birth of a new day

It's a new day, a new life
A harvest day, but a market day
To grow in knowledge and wisdom
In the strength and power of the creator
It's a new day with new hopes
To seek His face anew
To search for His footsteps and in them plant mine
To do what He would have me do
To say what He would have me say

It's a new day, a new hour, a new dawn
A new beginning with a fresh breath
New zests, faith and strength
New opportunities to listen, to hear and obey
His dictates, instructions and leadings
To live within the palms of His word
To abide by His laws and precepts
To reflect on His glory and splendor
To think on the fragrance, radiance and beauty of the kingdom

The success of the day is not to have achieved happiness
Accomplished a given task or met a desired goal
Nor to have avoided pains, sorrows and failures
But to have done the will of He who created the day
Live today like you would never live it again and thank God for the gift of a new day.

To The Angel Of Love

Your success is sky written above the clouds
Your victory is as plain as the sun in the sky
Your future is as bright as the morning star
He who has set you on the garden path
Would see you through!
See you in heaven!

Be My Bride

I see a young bride
Outfitted in a beautiful bridal gown
A divinely beautiful bride in golden colors
Satin-shoed, wearing an elbow length veil
Over a smiling radiant face
Stepping out in faith
Down the aisle, up the altar
Face to face with a groom, full of strength and vigor
A groom with a quest for divine truths
A consuming zeal for the things above

In faith we shall match forward to the altar
In love shall we alter our states from two to one
In His presence before the angelic hosts
We shall seal our love with a holy kiss
On the wings of His love
We shall ride off into the sunset
With His strength and by His grace
We shall scale the waves and stem the tides

Founded on faith and love
Called and chosen from the crowd by divine ordinance
Washed in that precious blood of His
Bound together in agape love
Perfected in holiness, clothed in righteousness
And shut up in the golden walls of His perfect will

Ours is a leap of faith
A reunion of love
A toast to life
A taste of paradise
Be my bride, says the Lord!

Why Mind The Thorns When You Can Pick The Roses?

Why do men race against the tide
Ignorantly trying to redefine life
When they know not how they came to be?

Why do men want to redirect the course of nature
Trying in vain to change the times and seasons
When they contributed nothing in the making of their own souls?

Just why do men shed innocent blood at will
Killing one another on the altars of Baal
When they know not when their own hour would come?

Why do men cheat, loot and steal
Storing up wealth beyond the needs of the soul
Saving goods and money for use after their poor souls' departure?

Why do men quarrel and fight
Pushing and scratching against one another, struggling to get into hell
When the train to heaven is a leisure ride?

Why do men gallivant the corners of the earth
Seeking for sins to do
Offering their spirits, their souls and bodies free to the devil to use at will?

Just why do men live like pigs in the mud
Refusing the free gift of love and life
When they can be robed in glory?

Why do you lie when it's easier to tell the truth
Crying, hurting and hating
When it's much better to love and rejoice?

Why do men enjoy sin deeds
When it's much more noble and most divine
To live right and be a saint?

Tell me: do you crawl when you can fly
Look at the mire when you can gaze at the stars
Or live like the dead amongst the living
When you can live above the stars?

Cry not when you can smile
Sigh not when you can sing and praise
Fret not when you can pray
And tell me: Why mind the thorns when you can pick the roses?

Time Is Running Out

The snows fall, inflicting deadly cold on mortal beings
The winds sigh, reminding us of the time we are in
The waters and deserts are shifting, warning us to be wise
As daylight dawns into darkness
And darkness into darkness
My heart bleeds for a dying world
Time is running out
Repent and be saved!

Christ Is Coming Soon

Hot and fierce, the wind blows
Across the darkening sky
Swift and steady time races by
Along life's track way
Soon, we would mount and ride
Into the gallery of heaven
The city where life reigns in splendor
There, our crowns lie unclaimed
Follow the spirit and make no room for the flesh
Christ is coming soon!

The End Is Near

Into the quiet of my heart
Comes a voice like an echo from above
Bringing home the healing waves of God's word
The joy and peace from on high
Shutting out the bitter sobs of a world in pains
The silent bleeds of multitudes in chains
Saying to all who cares to hear
The end is near!

The Racing Tide

Racing down life's sunless hill
The rich shall in their wealth find poverty
The wise in their wisdom find folly
The strong in their strength weakness
Yet, a moment more, just a little while longer
All shall be gone
Swept ashore, off the ocean of life
Forever lost in time and space
For time has reached its crest and life its summit!

Night Time Calls

The sky gets darker and darker
The clouds grow thicker and thicker
As the world becomes old, cold and bleak
The sun, the moon and the stars
With one voice chorus
The end is near!
Like a dying breeze life is drifting away
Soon, sooner than we think, the curtains would be drawn
As dark clouds cover the earth
What would be your story as night time calls?

Chapter Ten

The Voice From Above
—What Would Be Your Story?

A

The day is coming
The minutes are ticking away
Life is receding
Death is drawing near
Man is running to his grave
What would be your story?

The hour is approaching
When you shall hear the wake up call
The voice from above
Calling you to come
The soul shall journey through the dark tunnels of death
As the spirit departs the body without a parting kiss

The night shall come like a thief—dark and cold
The journey shall be short and brisk
When the heart strings shall be pulled from above
As the wind is taken out of your sail
And the tent of life is folded forever
What would be your story?

As the wheel of life comes to a permanent stop
All life's successes would be a distant echo
All achievements and titles a forgotten tale
All gold and grandeur a fading memory
Never again to claim
What would be your story?

Oh! The hour is forthcoming
The day brakes forth
That memorial day of reckoning
When you shall take a journey
Never to come back, never to look back
You shall sleep to wake no more
As the eyes are shut to all

On that fateful day, you shall speak no more
You shall see and hear no more
All knowledge and wisdom shall come to naught
Neither friend nor foe shall lift a voice
Neither sister nor brother shall lift a finger
You shall be there all alone, to be judged—damned or justified
Which would it be?

Your plight shall be beyond recall
Your fate beyond mercy
Your life beyond salvage
You would want to live again
If only to right the wrongs you've done to your soul
To undo the multitude of sins against man and God

You would plead and pray
You would shout and cry
"Give me back the life once mine"
"Give me one more chance"
But we all have just one life to live
One chance to make or mar
One spirit to ascend or descend

The seconds shall talk
The minutes would shout and tell
The days shall remember all and testify
For or against you
To damn and condemn
To justify, praise or reward
What would it be?

You shall know why you wouldn't live
Because you had never lived
The reason you must die
Because you had sold your life
To him who bought your soul
The evil one whom you served on earth

When the call is made for your soul
The angel of death would not tarry
It would be too late to effect a change of fate
Too late to live and be
Too late to repent of sinful deeds
To do good and live right

Today—heaven calls with an unquenchable love
Hell with smiling skulls sends invitation
Which would it be?
What do you want out of life?
Make your choice here before you become clay
There is no repentance after this phase
Make peace with God while you can

Nothing said ever goes unheard
Nothing done ever goes unseen
Nothing is hidden from he who knows us beyond the soul
The records would be there to show
All you ever said or did
All you ever failed to do or say

B:
This Shall Be My story

*L*ord, this shall be my story, my eternal report
I shall live the only way I know
By your laws and precepts
To know your grace of infinite mercy
Your blessings of limitless abundance
Your love that never fails

My soul shall be ready when you call
My spirit shall gladly come
With songs of victory to heaven's gates of gold
To receive the crown of life
Leaving this piece of clay behind
For them that need it

Christ came for me
For me He lived and died to pay all debts
For me He rose again to glory
Sealing my fate with His
Eagerly waiting for me to be done and come
To receive the rewards of faith in Him

I shall be clothed in glory
I shall be covered with a blanket of love
I shall receive the crown of days
I shall be given the kiss of life
To be, to live and never die
What would be your story?

As the cycle of life reaches its seventh
Time its final phase
One more lap to go
And the world would be as good as done
What would become of your soul
Beyond the funeral pyre
Above the silent slumber of death?

As darkest sighs exhale like vivid breath
As the sun presents a white ball gone black
As the earth divides to let in the wooden tray
Aside the anguish of mournful hearts
Over the funeral sighs, hymns and songs
What would be your story?

C:

As time runs to a final stop
And mankind her crest
The lions would cease to roar
The rains would cease to fall
The seasons would cease to come
For time has reached its zenith
Tell me friend, what would be your story?

In the heart of every man
Within the deep recesses of his mortal being
Beyond face, body and soul
Is an eternal diary
Wherein are written all he has done or failed to do
All he has said or failed to say
Therein lies the story of his life
What would be your story?

We are all locked within the den of time
Shut against the tide
But as life unwinds her coils
And all mortal strength is spent like waves on the seashore
Shall we emerge again to tell the story of life
What would be your story?
One soul is worth all the treasures the world can give
And one good word, one just deed is a treasure to your soul!